WNBA SUPERSTARS

COURTNEY VANDERSLOOT

by Jo-Ann Barnas

FOCUS READERS
NAVIGATOR

WWW.FOCUSREADERS.COM

Focus Readers is distributed by North Star Editions:
sales@northstareditions.com | 888-417-0195

Produced for Focus Readers by Red Line Editorial.

Photographs ©: Phelan M. Ebenhack/AP Images, cover, 1, 4–5, 7; Anthony Nesmith/Cal Sport Media/AP Images, 9; Denis Poroy/AP Images, 10–11; Elaine Thompson/AP Images, 13, 15; Damen Jackson/Cal Sport Media/AP Images, 16–17; Matt York/AP Images, 19; Ben Margot/AP Images, 21; Alex Brandon/AP Images, 22–23; Kamil Krzaczynski/AP Images, 24; Jeffrey Brown/Icon Sportswire/AP Images, 26; Eileen T. Meslar/AP Images, 28

Library of Congress Cataloging-in-Publication Data
Names: Barnas, Jo-Ann, author.
Title: Courtney Vandersloot / by Jo-Ann Barnas.
Description: Lake Elmo, MN : Focus Readers, [2022] | Series: WNBA Superstars | Includes index. | Audience: Grades 4-6
Identifiers: LCCN 2021040562 (print) | LCCN 2021040563 (ebook) | ISBN 9781637390726 (Hardcover) | ISBN 9781637391266 (Paperback) | ISBN 9781637391808 (eBook) | ISBN 9781637392287 (PDF)
Subjects: LCSH: Vandersloot, Courtney, 1989---Juvenile literature. | Women basketball players--United States--Biography--Juvenile literature. | Gonzaga Bulldogs (Basketball team)--Juvenile literature. | Basketball for women--United States--Juvenile literature. | Women's National Basketball Association--Juvenile literature.
Classification: LCC GV884.V368 B37 2022 (print) | LCC GV884.V368 (ebook) | DDC 796.323092 [B]--dc23
LC record available at https://lccn.loc.gov/2021040562
LC ebook record available at https://lccn.loc.gov/2021040563

Printed in the United States of America
Mankato, MN
012022

ABOUT THE AUTHOR

Jo-Ann Barnas spent the majority of her career as a sports feature writer in Detroit and Kansas City. Among her top personal athletic moments is being the shortest player to make the girls' basketball team in junior high.

TABLE OF CONTENTS

UChicago
Medicine
SPALDING

CHAPTER 1

RECORD-SETTING PLAYMAKER

The Chicago Sky were playing the Indiana Fever on August 31, 2020. It was late in the fourth quarter. Sky **point guard** Courtney Vandersloot already had 15 **assists** in the game. She'd recorded that many assists three other times in her career. But it had been 18 years since a Women's National Basketball

On August 18, 2020, Courtney Vandersloot was the first WNBA player to record at least 15 points, 15 assists, and 5 rebounds in one game.

Association (WNBA) player recorded 16 assists in a single game. That record had been achieved twice. WNBA great Ticha Penicheiro did it in 1998 and 2002.

Now, Vandersloot drove to the basket. She saw teammate Ruthy Hebard under the hoop. Vandersloot leaped as if she were going to shoot a layup. But she turned in midair and passed the ball instead. Hebard caught the pass. She put up the shot and scored. Her Sky teammates erupted in cheers. Vandersloot had just tied the WNBA record of 16 assists.

Vandersloot wasn't finished. Two minutes later, she passed to Allie

In 2020, Vandersloot became the first WNBA player to average double-digit assists over an entire season.

Quigley outside the paint. But Quigley was guarded quickly. So, she passed back to Vandersloot. Then the Sky's Stefanie Dolson set a **pick** for Quigley. That let Quigley get open in the corner. Vandersloot dished a pass to her. Quigley launched a three-point shot and scored.

There it was. Vandersloot had her 17th assist of the game. That was the most in league history. The 10-year **veteran** loved helping her teammates score. They loved that about her, too. Vandersloot was a true point guard. She was always looking out for everyone else.

Vandersloot had thought the record of 16 would last forever. But with help from Quigley, she'd broken it. The record meant a lot to both players. That's because Quigley was both Vandersloot's teammate and wife. When they married in 2018, the couple was the second active married couple in the league. For Vandersloot, the chance to team up with

Vandersloot (with ball) and Allie Quigley (far right) race downcourt on a fast break during a 2015 game.

her best friend on the record breaker was the cherry on top.

Before the game ended, Vandersloot earned one more assist. That extended her record to 18. The basket was scored on a three-pointer. Quigley hit the shot, of course.

GONZAGA
21

CHAPTER 2

SLOOT AND THE ZAGS

Courtney Vandersloot was born on February 8, 1989, in Kent, Washington. Courtney wasn't always into basketball. Her favorite sport growing up was soccer. She had a poster of soccer great Mia Hamm hanging on her bedroom wall. But by high school, Courtney had become hooked on basketball. She was

Courtney Vandersloot attempts a tough pass during a 2008 game with Gonzaga University.

a star, too. She became the state's top scorer in her last year at Kentwood High.

However, big-name colleges didn't pay much attention to Courtney. Some thought she was too small. But Gonzaga

JOHN STOCKTON

In Vandersloot's second year at Gonzaga, she decided to reach out to John Stockton. Stockton was in the NBA Hall of Fame. He was also considered the top men's point guard in Gonzaga history. Stockton was happy to help Vandersloot. He gave her tips. Their sessions together helped build her confidence. She'd thought plays such as one-handed passes were too risky. But Stockton showed her the power of confidence. With confidence, Vandersloot pulled off tough plays much more often.

Vandersloot makes a one-handed pass during a 2010 NCAA tournament game against Texas A&M.

University in her home state offered her a **scholarship**.

Vandersloot quickly made a name for herself. In her second year of college, she averaged 7.3 assists per game. That broke Gonzaga's school record. The next year, she broke her own record. She averaged

9.4 assists per game during the 2009–10 season. That was the best in the National Collegiate Athletic Association (NCAA).

Vandersloot was known for her no-look passes. She played like she was a step ahead of everyone else. Her talent helped put Gonzaga women's basketball on the map. Many fans came to see her play.

Her talent also turned Gonzaga into a winner. Nine years earlier, Gonzaga had posted a 0–14 record in the West Coast Conference. With Vandersloot, the Bulldogs went 14–0 in 2009–10.

Vandersloot kept improving. During her senior year, she became the first Division I player, male or female, to

Vandersloot drives to the basket during a 2011 NCAA tournament game against UCLA.

record 2,000 points and 1,000 assists in a career. Gonzaga advanced all the way to the NCAA Elite Eight. Vandersloot was named the best point guard in the United States. She was ready for the WNBA.

SKY
21
adidas
11

CHAPTER 3

PLAYING FOR THE SKY

Courtney Vandersloot's dreams of playing in the WNBA came true. The Chicago Sky made her the No. 3 overall pick in the 2011 **draft**. But playing in the WNBA wasn't going to be easy. In college, her team had won a lot. The Sky hadn't. In fact, Chicago had never reached the playoffs in its entire history.

Courtney Vandersloot puts up a jump shot in a 2011 WNBA game during her first season playing with the Chicago Sky.

Vandersloot played well in her first season. But she felt something was missing. So, she worked with a coach who lived in her home state. Vandersloot trained hard. She got stronger and gained more confidence. And, slowly, the Sky began to improve.

ALLIE QUIGLEY

Allie Quigley began her WNBA career in 2008. Her first years were a struggle. And in 2012, the Seattle Storm cut her. She missed the whole season as a result. In 2013, the Chicago Sky took a chance on Quigley. She met Vandersloot at the Sky's training camp. Five years later, the two married. They helped each other become better players. In 2019, Quigley made her third straight All-Star Game.

Vandersloot drives to the hoop during Game 2 of the 2014 WNBA Finals.

Chicago went 24–10 in 2013. That was the team's first-ever winning season. They made the playoffs for the first time, too. Vandersloot was in the middle of it all. She was third in the WNBA for assists. She also played aggressively on defense. The best was yet to come. But there were some challenges along the way.

The 2014 season began in mid-May. By late June, Vandersloot was out with a knee injury. She missed 17 games. The Sky made the playoffs, but just barely. By then, Vandersloot was back on the court.

Chicago beat Indiana in the Eastern Conference Finals. The victory sent the Sky to the WNBA Finals for the first time. Unfortunately, they lost to the Phoenix Mercury. Even so, there was nothing but smiles for the Sky. They had made it all the way to the championship.

SUE BIRD

Courtney Vandersloot was 13 years old when Sue Bird joined the WNBA in 2002. The point guards finally met in 2011 at a Team USA training camp. First-year Vandersloot was a sponge. That's because Bird was a seven-time All-Star for the Seattle Storm. Vandersloot watched and learned from everything Bird did. Five years later, they were together at another national team camp. This time it was Bird who sang Vandersloot's praises. But Vandersloot's eyes remained locked on her idol. She wanted to keep learning from the best.

In 2021, Sue Bird played her 18th season in the WNBA. She made her 12th All-Star team.

SKY
22
boost mobile

CHAPTER 4

RAISING HER GAME

In 2015, Courtney Vandersloot posted her best season to date. Her scoring average nearly doubled to a career-best 11.4 points per game. And for the second straight year, she led the league in assists. She even hit a personal milestone in June when she scored her 1,000th career point. On top of all of that,

Courtney Vandersloot soars for a shot during a 2015 game against the Washington Mystics.

Vandersloot dishes out a left-handed pass during a 2016 game against the Los Angeles Sparks.

Vandersloot started all 34 games for the first time in her career. By the end of the season, the Sky were back in the playoffs.

In the first game of the Eastern Conference semifinals, the Sky beat

Indiana 77–72. Vandersloot and Allie Quigley combined for 39 points in that game. But the Fever found a way to slow them down. Indiana won the next two games to clinch the playoff series.

The next two years were tough for Chicago. An injury caused Sky superstar Elena Delle Donne to miss the 2016 playoffs. Then Delle Donne was traded to the Washington Mystics in 2017. However, the loss of one superstar meant there was more room for another. Vandersloot stepped up.

Vandersloot had always been a terrific passer. Now she became a great shooter, too. In 2018, she recorded the first

Vandersloot passes to Allie Quigley during a 2019 game against the Indiana Fever.

triple-double in Sky history. Vandersloot recorded 13 points, 15 assists, and 10 rebounds against the Dallas Wings. Only six other players in league history had recorded a triple-double before.

By 2019, Vandersloot had helped rebuild the Sky into a playoff team. That season, she set a WNBA record with 9.1 assists per game. Chicago lost in the second round of the playoffs. But the Sky wanted to make sure Vandersloot wasn't going anywhere. So, in 2020, they signed her to a multiyear contract.

In 2020, Chicago was bounced from the playoffs in the first round. Still,

LIFE IN THE BUBBLE

During the 2020 season, all of the WNBA teams played in Florida. They lived there, too. That was because of the COVID-19 **pandemic**. Playing in a "bubble" helped keep players, staff, and fans safe. However, the bubble was tough for many players. They weren't able to be with friends or family for the whole season. The bubble was easier for Vandersloot. That was because she had Quigley at her side after practices and games.

At the 2021 All-Star break, Vandersloot had assisted in 47 percent of all the Sky's field goals that season.

Vandersloot came back strong in 2021. That season, she helped the Sky reach the Finals. Vandersloot averaged 12.5 assists per game in the series. Chicago came out on top, and Vandersloot won her first WNBA championship!

COURTNEY VANDERSLOOT

- Height: 5 feet 8 inches (173 cm)
- Weight: 145 pounds (66 kg)
- Birth date: February 8, 1989
- Birthplace: Kent, Washington
- High school: Kentwood High School (Covington, Washington)
- College: Gonzaga University (Spokane, Washington) (2007–2011)
- Pro team: Chicago Sky (2011–)
- Major awards: WNBA All-Star (2011, 2019, 2021); WNBA champion (2021)

FOCUS ON
COURTNEY VANDERSLOOT

Write your answers on a separate piece of paper.

1. Write a paragraph that explains the main idea of Chapter 2.
2. Would you want to play point guard? Why or why not?
3. What year did the Chicago Sky make their first WNBA Finals?

   A. 2011
   B. 2014
   C. 2020

4. Why is a point guard considered to be a leader on the court?

   A. The point guard always takes the most shots.
   B. The point guard blocks the most shots.
   C. The point guard helps others on the team score.

Answer key on page 32.

GLOSSARY

assists

Passes that lead directly to a teammate scoring.

draft

A system that allows teams to acquire new players coming into a league.

pandemic

A disease that spreads quickly around the world.

pick

A move where a player blocks a defender, allowing a teammate to pass or drive.

point guard

The player on a basketball team who runs the team's offense.

scholarship

Money given to a student to pay for education expenses.

triple-double

A game in which a player has double-digit numbers in three categories. The categories are often points, assists, and rebounds.

veteran

A person who has been doing his or her job for a long time and has a lot of experience.

TO LEARN MORE

BOOKS

Buckey, A. W. *Women in Basketball.* Lake Elmo, MN: Focus Readers, 2020.

Hoehn, Jim. *WNBA*. Minneapolis: Abdo Publishing, 2021.

Omoth, Tyler. *The WNBA Finals.* North Mankato, MN: Capstone Press, 2020.

NOTE TO EDUCATORS

Visit **www.focusreaders.com** to find lesson plans, activities, links, and other resources related to this title.

INDEX

Answer Key: 1. Answers will vary; **2.** Answers will vary; **3.** B; **4.** C